IF YOU CAN TEXT, YOU CAN VIBE CODE

Build Real Apps Just by Talking to AI
No Tech Skills Required

REBECCA M. STALLWORTH

If You Can Text, You Can Vibe Code
Build Real Apps Just by Talking to AI—No Tech Skills Required

ISBN: 979-8-218-92838-4

Published by Rebecca M. Stallworth
Prince George's County, Maryland

First Edition: 2026

Affiliate Disclosure: Some links in this book are affiliate links. The author may earn a commission at no extra cost to you.

For my mother,
who taught me to keep moving forward

And for my son Joshua,
onward is always the move for us

Foreword

When my mom told me I needed to build a SaaS or an app, I'll be honest—I wasn't interested.

I already had a business. Gosh Josh Cookies was my thing, something I built from scratch, something I was proud of. But to take it to the next level, I needed capital. And my mom, being who she is, wasn't about to just hand me the money. She challenged me to earn it by creating something new—a software product.

That's how she's always been. Being homeschooled by her, I learned early that she presents challenges and opportunities constantly. Some of them I'm into. Some of them I'm not. This one? At first, I definitely was not.

But then one weekend, something clicked.

I started talking to ChatGPT and Claude, just exploring what was possible. My mom told me to take one of my hobbies—either flying or sailing—and think about what needs improvement. What's frustrating? What's harder than it should be?

I thought about my last sailing trip in the summer of 2025, a few days on the Chesapeake Bay. And I remembered all the pain points. The things that didn't work. The frustrations that everyone just accepted as normal.

That was my eureka moment.

I realized I could actually build something to solve those problems. Not someday. Not after getting a degree or saving up to hire developers. Right now, by just describing what I needed.

My life has been different ever since.

If you're holding this book, you're about to discover the same thing I did: you don't need permission to build. You don't need to be technical. You just need an idea and the willingness to describe it clearly.

My mom wrote this book to show you how. Trust me—if it clicked for me on a random weekend, it can click for you too.

Joshua Stallworth

Founder, Gosh Josh Cookies

START BUILDING IN THE NEXT 60 SECONDS

Want to experience vibe coding before you even finish this book?

Scan the QR code below to open CreateAnything—a tool that lets you build real mobile apps just by describing what you want. No downloads. No setup. Just scan and start creating.

By the time you finish the first few chapters, you could already have your first app running on your phone. Seriously.

createanything.com

Tip

This isn't just a preview—it's the real deal. Readers who scan this code and follow along while reading consistently build better projects than those who just read passively. Try it.

Contents

Introduction

My Journey to Vibe Coding

I've been building websites for years. It started back when I was homeschooling my son, Joshua. I taught myself WordPress, figured out Shopify, and spent countless hours piecing together websites for various projects and side hustles.

My aha moment came when I discovered I could buy themes. Suddenly, I didn't have to design everything from scratch. I could purchase a professional theme, customize it, and have something that looked polished without needing a design degree. That was a game changer for me.

I got ambitious. I thought, 'What if I could create and sell my own themes?' I dove deeper into coding, trying to level up my skills enough to build themes other people would pay for. But the learning curve was steep. The more I learned, the more I realized how much more I needed to learn. Eventually, I lost motivation. Life got busy, and the dream of a theme business faded into the background.

Fast forward to this school year. Joshua is now a business major in college, and I challenged him: 'You cannot finish this school year without having built a real product.' I sent him YouTube videos, TikTok clips, articles about entrepreneurs building software. I gave him feedback on his ideas. I wanted him to understand that you don't need to wait for permission or a job to create something valuable.

In 2025, Joshua and I started experimenting with AI tools together. I was using ChatGPT to help me debug problems with my existing sites, and I stumbled across YouTube videos showing people using AI to build entire applications.

Now, let me be honest—at first, it was still a process. Using ChatGPT to code wasn't seamless. There was back-and-forth, troubleshooting, moments of frustration. It was helpful, but it wasn't magic.

But then I watched a video that changed my perspective.

> I watched someone describe an app in plain English and watched AI build it in minutes. No complex syntax. No cryptic error messages. Just a conversation.

That's when I realized the tools had crossed a threshold. It wasn't perfect, but it was good enough to actually ship real projects. And compared to the old days of Stack Overflow rabbit holes and documentation that assumed you already knew everything? It was revolutionary.

Then I discovered Claude Code. And that changed everything.

Claude Code is, in my opinion, a beast of a tool. The way it understands context, writes clean code, and actually helps you build real projects—it's on another level. I went from experimenting to actually shipping things. Real tools. Real solutions. Things that work.

My goal through all of this has been clear: I want to transition from being a public school teacher into entrepreneurship full-time. I love teaching—I teach art by day and college history by night—but I know there's more for me. I've been building toward that exit for years through my Etsy shop, my writing, my various projects. Vibe coding is the piece that makes building real software products finally accessible.

What Is Vibe Coding?

The term 'vibe coding' was coined by Andrej Karpathy, a brilliant computer scientist who worked on Tesla's self-driving technology and some of the most advanced AI systems in the world. When someone like that says something fundamental has changed, it's worth paying attention.

Here's the idea: Instead of writing code line by line with precise syntax, you describe what you want in natural language. You explain the vibe—the feeling, the function, the goal—and AI handles the technical translation.

Tip

Think of it like describing a meal to a chef. You don't need to know how to julienne vegetables or make a roux. You describe what you're in the mood for, and someone with those skills makes it happen. Vibe coding works the same way—AI has the technical skills, you provide the vision.

You might say things like:

"Create a simple website for my tutoring business with a booking calendar and contact form."

"Build me an app that tracks my daily habits and shows my streaks."

"I need a tool where parents can sign up for conference time slots."

The AI reads your description, understands what you're asking for, and generates working code. Within minutes, you have something real—not a sketch or mockup, but an actual functioning application.

Why This Book Exists

Most resources about vibe coding are written for people who already know how to code. They assume you understand 'APIs' and 'frontend frameworks' and 'deployment pipelines.' They're aimed at developers who want to work faster, not regular people who want to build something from scratch.

This book is different.

I wrote it for people like me—people who have been building things online for years but hit walls when it came to 'real' software. People who have ideas but thought they needed a computer science degree or thousands of dollars to hire a developer. Teachers, small business owners, parents, side hustlers, anyone who's ever thought 'I wish there was an app for that' and felt stuck.

I wrote it for my son Joshua and his generation of entrepreneurs who shouldn't have to wait for permission to build.

And honestly? I wrote it for myself—to document what I've learned and share the tools that are helping me build toward the life I want.

What You'll Learn

By the end of this book, you'll have built real projects:

- A personal website — Your own corner of the internet
- A web application — Something that actually does things and solves problems
- A mobile app — Something that lives on your phone
- A product you could sell — A foundation for potential income

More importantly, you'll understand how to communicate with AI to build almost anything you can imagine. The specific tools will evolve—that's guaranteed—but the skill of clearly describing what you want will only become more valuable.

A Note on Affiliate Links

Some links in this book are affiliate links. If you sign up for a tool through my link, I may earn a small commission at no extra cost to you. I only recommend tools I actually use and believe in. I'll always be transparent about these relationships.

Now let's get started. Your first app is closer than you think.

1   The Old World vs. The New World

What Building Software Used to Require

Let me paint a picture of what creating an app looked like just a few years ago—before AI changed everything. Understanding where we came from helps you appreciate just how dramatically the landscape has shifted.

First, you needed to learn a programming language. Not just one, actually—you typically needed several. HTML for the structure of web pages (what elements exist and where they go). CSS for making them look nice (colors, fonts, spacing, layouts). JavaScript for making them interactive (what happens when you click buttons, how forms work, how content updates without refreshing the page).

Then maybe Python or Ruby or PHP for the backend—the behind-the-scenes stuff that handles data and logic. And if you wanted to build a mobile app? Add Swift for iPhones and Kotlin or Java for Android. Each platform had its own language, its own rules, its own ecosystem.

Each of these languages has its own syntax, its own quirks, its own way of doing things. They have different rules for how you structure code, different patterns for common tasks, different communities with different conventions. Even punctuation matters—miss a semicolon or use the wrong type of bracket, and everything breaks.

Learning just one of these languages well enough to build something functional takes months of dedicated study. Learning all of them? Years. And that's assuming you have the time and motivation to push through the frustration of debugging cryptic error messages and the existential despair of watching your code fail for reasons you don't understand.

But language was just the beginning. You also needed to understand:

- Frameworks — Pre-built structures that help you organize your code. React, Angular, Vue, Django, Rails, Laravel, and dozens more. Each with their own philosophy, their own way of doing things, their own learning curve. Pick the wrong one and you might have to start over.

- Databases — Where your app stores information permanently. SQL vs. NoSQL. PostgreSQL vs. MySQL vs. MongoDB. Tables and schemas and queries and migrations. Understanding how to structure data efficiently is almost a discipline unto itself.

- APIs — How different systems talk to each other. REST vs. GraphQL. Authentication tokens. Rate limiting. Error handling. If you wanted your app to send emails or process payments or check the weather, you needed to understand how to communicate with external services.

- Servers — Where your app actually lives and runs. Linux administration. Cloud providers like AWS or Google Cloud or Azure. Containers and Docker and Kubernetes. Scaling and load balancing. Making sure your app doesn't crash when too many people use it at once.

- Version control — How to track changes to your code over time. Git, branches, merges, pull requests. Essential for any real project, especially if you're working with others.

- Deployment — How to get your finished app onto the internet so people can actually use it. CI/CD pipelines. Hosting configurations. Domains and DNS settings. SSL certificates for security.

- Security — How to keep hackers out and user data safe. Encryption, authentication, authorization. SQL injection, cross-site scripting, CSRF attacks. The OWASP guidelines. One mistake could expose your users' private information to the world.

And that's just the technical stuff. You also needed:

- Time — Lots and lots of time. Building even a simple app from scratch could take weeks or months of dedicated work. Complex apps? Years.
- Patience — To deal with bugs that make no sense, error messages that seem designed to confuse, and the inevitable moment when everything breaks for no apparent reason at 11 PM when you just want to go to sleep.
- Money — For courses, books, tools, hosting, and all the other expenses that add up. A coding bootcamp could cost $10,000-$20,000. Self-teaching was cheaper but required even more time.
- A certain kind of brain — Or so people thought. The myth persisted that programming required a special type of intelligence that only some people possessed. You either 'got it' or you didn't.

The message was clear: Building software is for professionals. For tech people. For a specific type of person who enjoys spending hours staring at incomprehensible text on a black screen, who finds satisfaction in tracking down a missing comma that broke everything, who speaks in jargon that sounds like a foreign language to everyone else.

If that wasn't you? Too bad. Come back with a computer science degree or a few thousand dollars for a developer.

The Gatekeepers

For decades, there were gatekeepers standing between regular people and the ability to build software. These gatekeepers weren't malicious—they were just the natural result of how complex software development had become.

Educational gatekeepers: Universities and coding bootcamps that cost thousands of dollars and required months or years of commitment. Self-teaching was possible, but it required tremendous discipline and often led to gaps in knowledge. Without a structured curriculum, how would you know what you didn't know?

Technical gatekeepers: The sheer complexity of the tools and technologies required. Even 'beginner' tutorials assumed a level of comfort with computers that many people didn't have. 'Just open your terminal' — what's a terminal? 'Clone the repository' — what's a repository? The jargon itself was a barrier.

Financial gatekeepers: The cost of hiring developers if you couldn't code yourself. Even simple apps could cost $5,000-$50,000, putting software development out of reach for most individuals and small organizations. Got a great idea for an app? Better start saving.

Cultural gatekeepers: The tech industry's reputation for being unwelcoming to outsiders, with its jargon, its inside jokes, and its sometimes-hostile online communities. Ask a 'stupid question' and you might get mocked instead of helped. The culture could feel exclusive, like a club you weren't invited to join.

These gatekeepers didn't exist because anyone wanted to keep people out (well, mostly). They existed because building software was genuinely hard. The skills required were real and took real time to develop. The complexity wasn't artificial.

But then something happened that changed everything.

The Great Democratization

In late 2022, OpenAI released ChatGPT to the public—and the world shifted on its axis.

ChatGPT wasn't the first AI, and it wasn't even the first language model. Researchers had been working on this technology for years. But it was the first one that regular people could use easily, the first one that felt genuinely intelligent in conversation, and—crucially—the first one that could understand natural language AND understand code.

It could translate between the two.

Suddenly, you didn't need to speak the computer's language. The computer could finally speak yours.

This was the beginning of vibe coding, though nobody called it that yet. People started discovering they could describe what they wanted in plain English, and the AI would write the code for them. Want a function that calculates compound interest? Just ask. Need to sort a list of names alphabetically? Just describe it.

Early on, this was helpful but limited. You'd get code, but then you had to figure out what to do with it. Where does it go? How do you run it? How do you put it on the internet for other people to use? The code was often incomplete, and making different pieces work together still required technical knowledge.

Then came the next wave: AI-powered app builders that handled everything.

Platforms emerged that let you describe what you want, generated the code automatically, AND handled all the technical infrastructure. No copying and pasting code into mysterious files. No figuring out servers or databases. No deployment headaches.

Just describe what you want, watch it get built, and share it with the world.

The gatekeepers haven't disappeared entirely—complex projects still benefit from professional developers, and there are still things AI can't do well. But the gates are now open for anyone who wants to walk through them. The barrier to entry has dropped from years of study to an afternoon of experimentation.

What Matters Now

In the new world of vibe coding, the most important skill isn't knowing how to write code—it's knowing how to communicate clearly.

Think about that for a second. The skill that matters most for building technology is the same skill that matters for writing a good email, giving clear directions, or explaining something to a friend. It's communication.

- Can you describe what you want?
- Can you be specific about details?
- Can you give feedback when something isn't quite right?
- Can you break down a big idea into smaller pieces?

If you can do any of that—and you can, because you do it every day in normal conversation—you can vibe code.

> **Tip**
> Think of it like driving a car. You don't need to understand how an internal combustion engine works, or how the transmission shifts gears, or how the anti-lock braking system prevents skids. You just need to know how to steer, accelerate, and brake. The car handles the complex mechanical stuff. Vibe coding tools work the same way—they handle the complex technical stuff while you steer.

The technical knowledge isn't gone—it's just been absorbed by the AI. The code still exists. The databases still get created. The servers still run. But you don't need to manage any of it directly. You provide the direction—the what and the why. The AI handles the how.

This is a fundamental shift. For the first time in the history of computing, you can build real software without learning to code. Not toy projects or limited templates—real, functional, custom applications built to your specifications.

Who Benefits Most

This shift benefits almost everyone who has ideas but lacked the technical means to execute them. Some groups benefit especially:

- Small business owners who need custom tools but can't justify developer costs. You know your business better than any outside developer ever could. Now you can build your own appointment scheduler, inventory tracker, customer feedback system, or whatever else you need. When you want to change something, you change it—no waiting for a developer's availability or paying for their time.

• Teachers who have ideas for educational apps and classroom tools. You see gaps that ed-tech companies miss. You know what would actually help your students. Now you can build it.

• Nonprofit workers who need better systems but have limited budgets. When every dollar counts and there's no budget for custom software, being able to build your own tools is transformative. Volunteer coordination, donation tracking, event management—build what you need.

• Retirees with time and ideas but no interest in learning to code. Your decades of experience and wisdom can now become software. That system you always wished existed? Build it.

• Side hustlers who want to build passive income streams. Software products can generate revenue while you sleep. What used to require either coding skills or a development budget is now accessible.

• Parents who need family organization tools. Chore trackers, allowance managers, family calendars, homework helpers—build exactly what your family needs, customized to how you actually live.

• Church and community volunteers who need better sign-up systems, event management, and communication tools. No more wrestling with generic software that doesn't quite fit your needs.

• Anyone with an idea who was previously locked out of the ability to build it. The democratization is real, and it's for everyone.

If you've ever said 'I wish there was an app that...' and then felt stuck because you couldn't build it yourself, vibe coding is your answer.

The Honest Truth: What Vibe Coding Can't Do (Yet)

Now, let me be honest with you. Vibe coding is powerful, but it's not magic. There are limitations you should know about upfront, so you have realistic expectations:

- Simple to medium-complexity projects work best. The more complex your app, the more likely you'll hit limitations. Building a basic website? Easy. A scheduling tool? Definitely doable. A customer portal with a few features? Absolutely. But building a complex enterprise system with dozens of user roles, intricate permission systems, and integration with legacy corporate systems? That still benefits from professional developers. The good news: what counts as 'simple' keeps expanding. Things that were impossible to vibe-code a year ago are straightforward now.

- You'll still need to iterate. The AI rarely gets everything perfect on the first try. You'll describe what you want, see what it builds, and then describe adjustments. This back-and-forth is normal and actually part of what makes it work. It's a conversation, not a single command. Don't expect perfection immediately—expect collaboration.

- Some coding knowledge helps (but isn't required). You can absolutely vibe code with zero technical background—that's the whole point. But having a basic understanding of concepts like 'database' or 'user authentication' makes communicating with AI easier. Don't worry—I'll teach you the concepts you need as we go. You'll pick them up naturally.

- Tools change fast. What works today might be different tomorrow. The specific platforms I mention in this book may evolve, add features, change pricing, or even disappear. But the principles remain. Learning to communicate clearly with AI is a skill that transfers across tools.

• Not everything is free. Most vibe coding tools offer free tiers that are quite capable, but serious projects may require paid plans. Building something for yourself to use? Probably free. Building something for hundreds of users? Expect to pay something. I'll be clear about costs as we go through each tool.

None of these limitations are deal-breakers. They're just reality. Knowing them upfront will save you frustration later and help you choose the right projects to tackle.

Your New Superpowers

Let's end this chapter on a high note. Here's what you're gaining by learning to vibe code:

• Speed — Build in hours what used to take weeks or months. Ideas can become reality the same day you have them. That scheduling tool I'd been dreaming about for years? Built in an afternoon. The speed fundamentally changes what's possible.

• Independence — No more waiting on developers or depending on tech-savvy friends and family members. No more begging your nephew who 'knows computers' to help you. You can do it yourself, on your own timeline.

• Iteration — Try ideas quickly and cheaply. If something doesn't work, pivot to something else. Test concepts before investing significant time or money. Failure becomes cheap and fast instead of expensive and slow.

• Empowerment — Join conversations about technology from a position of understanding, not confusion. You'll never feel intimidated by tech talk again. When someone mentions 'the frontend' or 'the database,' you'll know what they mean.

• Opportunity — Build tools for yourself, for your community, or even for sale. New doors are opening. Income streams that required technical skills or development budgets are now accessible to anyone with good ideas and clear communication.

The playing field has leveled. You don't need permission, credentials, or a technical background to build software anymore. You just need an idea and the ability to describe it.

Ready to learn how? Let's look at the tools that make all of this possible.

2 Your Vibe Coding Toolkit

The Tools That Make This Possible

Before we start building, let's get familiar with the tools you'll use. Think of this chapter as a tour of your new workshop. I'll introduce each tool, explain what it's good for, and help you understand when to use which one.

Don't worry about memorizing everything right now. You'll get hands-on experience with each tool in later chapters. For now, just get a sense of what's available. Bookmark this chapter—you'll probably come back to it as a reference.

The Conversational AI Assistants

These are the general-purpose AI assistants that started the revolution. They're your brainstorming partners and problem-solvers.

ChatGPT — chat.openai.com

OpenAI's conversational AI for brainstorming, writing, and code help

> *Best for: Quick answers, debugging, brainstorming ideas*
> *| Cost: Free / $20/mo*

ChatGPT is probably the AI you've heard most about. It's great for quick questions, brainstorming, and getting help with code problems. I've used it to debug issues on my existing websites—describe the problem, paste the error message, and it usually points me in the right direction.

The free tier is capable for most tasks. ChatGPT Plus ($20/month) gives you access to the latest models and faster responses during busy times.

Claude — claude.ai

Anthropic's AI assistant known for nuanced understanding and longer conversations

Best for: Deep thinking, complex problems, detailed explanations | Cost: Free / $20/mo

Claude (made by Anthropic) is ChatGPT's main competitor. In my experience, Claude excels at nuanced conversations and understanding complex context. When I need to think through something complicated or want a more detailed explanation, Claude is often my go-to.

Claude Code: My Favorite Discovery

I need to give Claude Code its own section because it deserves it. This tool is a beast.

Claude Code — claude.ai (Code feature)

AI-powered coding environment that builds complete projects from descriptions

Best for: Building full applications, complex features, professional results | Cost: Included with Claude Pro

Claude Code isn't just an AI that helps you write code—it's an AI that builds with you. You describe what you want, and it creates complete, working code. But what sets it apart is how it handles complexity and context.

When I started using Claude Code, I went from experimenting to actually shipping real projects. The difference was night and day compared to my earlier attempts with other tools. It understands what you're trying to accomplish, writes clean code, and can handle multi-step projects without losing track of what you're building.

Why I Love Claude Code

What makes Claude Code special: • Understands complex, multi-part requests • Maintains context across long conversations • Writes professional-quality code • Explains

If you're serious about vibe coding, I highly recommend trying Claude Code. It's included with Claude Pro ($20/month), and in my opinion, it's worth every penny.

The Instant App Builders

These platforms combine AI with everything needed to actually run your app. You describe what you want, and they don't just generate code—they create a working application you can see, use, and share immediately.

Lovable — lovable.dev

AI app builder with beautiful designs, built-in database, and one-click deployment

Best for: Beautiful web apps, fast development, polished results | Cost: Free / ~$20/mo

Lovable is specifically designed for vibe coding. It's built around the idea that you should be able to describe an app and get a working result—not just code, but a complete, deployed application.

What makes Lovable great for beginners:

- Extremely fast—often under a minute to see your first version
- Beautiful default designs that look professional
- Built-in database and user authentication
- One-click deployment with a shareable link
- You can export your code if you ever want to move elsewhere

Important

Affiliate Note: Lovable has an affiliate program. If you sign up through links I share, I may earn a commission at no extra cost to you. I recommend Lovable because I genuinely think it's excellent for beginners, not just because of the affiliate relationship.

Replit — replit.com

Coding platform with AI assistant that works on any device including phones

Best for: Learning, experimenting, coding anywhere, collaboration | Cost: Free / ~$25/mo

Replit has been around for years as a collaborative coding platform, but their AI features have transformed it. Their 'Replit Agent' can build entire applications from a description.

What makes Replit unique:

- Works on any device, including your phone—code from anywhere
- Great for beginners who want to learn concepts alongside building
- Built-in hosting—your app goes live automatically
- Large community with templates and examples
- More transparent about what's happening technically (good for learning)

Bolt.new — bolt.new

Fast web app builder focused on speed and simplicity

Best for: Quick prototypes, testing ideas fast, MVPs | Cost: Free tier available

Bolt.new is great for getting ideas out quickly. When you want to test whether a concept works before investing more time, Bolt helps you see results fast.

The Mobile App Maker

Want to build an iPhone app that people can download from the App Store? Something with an icon on their home screen? This is where CreateAnything shines.

CreateAnything — createanything.com

Build native iPhone and web apps with one-click App Store submission

Best for: Mobile apps, App Store publishing, cross-platform | Cost: Free / ~$16/mo

Most vibe coding tools focus on web applications. CreateAnything is different—it builds native mobile apps that you can actually submit to Apple's App Store.

Key features:

- Build real iPhone AND Android apps, not just websites
- Preview on your actual phone as you build
- One-click submission to the App Store
- Built-in payments through Stripe
- The AI actually fixes its own errors as it builds

The Power Tool: Cursor

Cursor is for when you want more control. It's an AI-powered code editor—think of it as a power tool for when you're ready to go deeper.

Cursor — cursor.com

AI-powered code editor for more control and complex projects

Best for: Advanced users, complex projects, learning code | Cost: Free / $20/mo

You might wonder: 'I thought the point was NOT to deal with code?' Here's the thing—as you get comfortable with vibe coding, you might want more control. You might want to understand what's happening under the hood or make precise tweaks.

Cursor meets you there. It's a code editor with AI deeply integrated. You can ask it to write code, explain code, or modify existing code. Many vibe coders start with simpler tools and graduate to Cursor as they gain confidence.

Choosing the Right Tool

With all these options, how do you choose? Here's a simple guide:

Quick Decision Guide

'I want to brainstorm or debug something' → ChatGPT or Claude 'I want to build a complete project with AI' → Claude Code 'I want a web app, fast and beautiful' → Lovable 'I want to learn while building' → Replit 'I want a quick prototype' → Bolt.new 'I want an iPhone/Android app' → CreateAnything 'I want full control over code' → Cursor

In practice, you'll often use multiple tools together. You might brainstorm with Claude, build in Lovable, and use Claude Code for complex features. There's no single 'right' choice—just the right tool for what you're doing right now.

Setting Up Your Accounts

Before moving on, create free accounts on these platforms:

- Claude (claude.ai) — Your AI thinking partner and coding assistant
- Lovable (lovable.dev) — Your main app builder for web applications
- Replit (replit.com) — Your backup builder and learning environment
- CreateAnything (createanything.com) — For when you want mobile apps

All have free tiers that let you follow along with everything in this book. You can upgrade later if needed.

Ready? Let's learn how to talk to these tools effectively. The next chapter teaches the most important skill in vibe coding: writing prompts that get results.

3 The Art of the Prompt

The Skill That Changes Everything

The single most important skill in vibe coding isn't technical—it's communication. The quality of what you build depends almost entirely on how well you describe what you want.

This chapter teaches you how to write prompts that get results. Master this, and you'll be able to build almost anything. Skip it or skim it, and you'll spend hours frustrated by results that aren't what you wanted.

I'm going to be honest: when I first started vibe coding, I thought I could just type a few words and get exactly what I wanted. 'Make me an app' seemed like enough. I was wrong. The AI did make something, but it wasn't what I had in mind. The difference between my imagination and what appeared on screen was frustrating.

Then I learned to write better prompts, and everything changed. The same AI that had frustrated me started producing exactly what I wanted—sometimes better than what I'd imagined. The tool didn't change. My communication did.

What Is a Prompt?

A prompt is simply what you type to the AI. It's your request, your description, your instructions. The word comes from theater—a prompt is what helps an actor know what to say next. In the same way, your prompt helps the AI know what to create.

When you tell ChatGPT 'Write a poem about a sunset,' that's a prompt. When you tell Lovable 'Create a website for my bakery,' that's a prompt too. Any input you give to an AI system to get output is a prompt.

> Bad prompts get bad results. Good prompts get good results.
> Great prompts get results that make you say 'Wow, that's
> exactly what I wanted.' The difference isn't luck—it's skill, and it
> can be learned.

Let's learn to write great prompts.

The Five Elements of a Great Prompt

After writing thousands of prompts and seeing what works,
I've identified five elements that consistently lead to great
results. You don't always need all five, but including more of
them usually produces better outcomes.

Element 1: Be Specific About What You Want

Vague prompts produce vague results. The AI has to
guess at anything you don't specify, and it often guesses
wrong—not because it's stupid, but because there are many
reasonable interpretations of vague requests.

Compare these prompts:

> *"Make me a website."*

This could produce literally anything—a blog, a portfolio,
a business site, a social network. The AI will pick something,
but it's essentially random from your perspective.

> *"Make me a website for my bakery."*

Better! Now the AI knows the context. But which bakery?
What kind? What should the website include?

> *"Make me a website for Sweet Delights Bakery in Atlanta. We*
> *specialize in custom cakes and French pastries for special*
> *occasions like weddings and birthdays. The site needs our*
> *menu with prices, a photo gallery of our work, contact*
> *information including our address and hours, and a form for*
> *customers to request custom cake quotes."*

Now we're talking! The AI knows exactly what to build. It
understands the business, the offerings, the location, and

the specific features needed. The result will be dramatically better.

The more specific you are, the less the AI has to guess—and the better your results will be.

Element 2: Describe the User

Who will use what you're building? Telling the AI helps it make appropriate design and functionality decisions. An app for teenagers looks and works differently than an app for retirees. An internal tool for employees is different from a public website for customers.

"Build a scheduling app."

For whom? The AI will make assumptions that might be completely wrong for your actual users.

"Build a scheduling app for elderly users at a senior center. They're not very comfortable with technology, so everything needs to be simple with large text, clear buttons with plenty of space between them, and no confusing options. They'll use it to sign up for activities like bingo, exercise classes, and movie nights."

Now the AI knows to prioritize simplicity and accessibility. It will make design choices that serve those specific users—larger fonts, higher contrast, simpler navigation, more forgiving touch targets.

Tip

Think about your actual users. Are they tech-savvy or beginners? Young or old? Using phones or computers? In a hurry or taking their time? Internal team members or public customers? These details shape what you build.

Element 3: Explain the Purpose

Why does this need to exist? What problem does it solve? Understanding the purpose helps the AI make smarter decisions about features and design. Sometimes it will even suggest things you didn't think to ask for because it understands the underlying goal.

"Create a form for my church."

A form for what? Membership? Donations? Prayer requests? Event signup? The AI is flying blind.

> *"Our church needs a way for members to sign up to bring food to our monthly potluck. Right now we use paper sign-ups passed around during service, and things fall through the cracks—sometimes we end up with ten desserts and no main dishes, or too much food one month and not enough the next. I need a form that shows what food categories still need items so people can see gaps and fill them before we end up unbalanced."*

Now the AI understands the actual problem: coordinating potluck contributions and avoiding imbalances. It might add features you didn't explicitly request—like showing how many items are signed up in each category, or sending reminders, or creating a summary list for the organizer.

When you explain the 'why,' the AI can be a better collaborator, not just a tool that follows orders.

Element 4: Specify Features

What does your app actually need to do? List the features explicitly. The more specific you are about functionality, the more likely you'll get what you need on the first try.

Good Feature List

I need an app to track my water intake. Features should include: - A big, easy-to-tap button to log each glass of water - A daily goal I can customize (default to 8 glasses) - A visual progress bar or indicator showing how close I am to my goal - Reminders every 2 hours during waking hours (8am-10pm) - A weekly summary showing my average daily intake - The ability to see my history for the past 30 days - A simple, calming design that doesn't feel clinical

Don't worry about being too detailed. It's much easier for the AI to ignore unnecessary details than to guess at missing ones. If you're not sure whether to include something, include it. You can always remove features later; it's harder to add them if the foundation wasn't built with them in mind.

Element 5: Describe the Look and Feel

How should it look? What's the vibe? (Yes, the vibe matters in vibe coding—that's partly where the name comes from.) The aesthetic and emotional tone of your app matter, and you can guide them with your words.

> *"The design should be clean and minimal, with calming blue and green colors. It should feel friendly and encouraging, not clinical or harsh. Modern but not trendy—I want it to still look good in a year, not like it's chasing the latest design fad."*

Or completely different:

> *"Make it look professional and corporate—this is for a law firm. Navy blue and gold colors. Conservative, serif fonts. Nothing playful or casual. It should inspire confidence and trust."*

Or something else entirely:

> *"Fun and playful, with bright colors and rounded shapes. This is for kids, so it should feel like a game, not like homework. Include some animations that make interactions feel satisfying."*

The AI can adopt almost any aesthetic. Your job is to tell it what you want. Don't assume it will guess correctly—describe the feeling you're going for.

The Magic Formula

Here's a template you can use for almost any project. It combines all five elements into a single, comprehensive prompt:

The Perfect Prompt Template
I want to build [WHAT] for [WHO] because [WHY]. It needs to [FEATURES]. The look should be [AESTHETIC].

Let me show you this formula in action with a real example:

> *"I want to build a volunteer scheduling system for our community food bank because right now everything is done through email and spreadsheets, and it's chaotic—shifts get*

double-booked, sometimes nobody shows up because they forgot, and coordinators spend hours every week just managing the schedule. Volunteers should be able to see available shifts for the upcoming two weeks, sign up for shifts that work with their schedule, get automatic email reminders 24 hours before their shift, and cancel if something comes up (which should free the spot for someone else). Coordinators should be able to create new shifts, see who's signed up for each one, get alerts when shifts are understaffed, send messages to all volunteers, and export the weekly schedule to print or share. The look should be warm and welcoming—we want volunteers to feel appreciated, not processed. Use friendly colors, nothing cold or corporate. It should work well on phones since most volunteers will access it that way."

That's a prompt that will produce something useful on the first try. It takes more time to write, but it saves enormous time on iteration and revision. The few minutes you spend on a thorough prompt can save hours of back-and-forth.

Starting Simple, Adding Complexity

Here's a liberating secret: You don't have to get everything right in your first prompt.

Vibe coding is conversational. You describe something, the AI builds it, you see the result, and then you describe changes. It's a dialogue, not a monologue. The AI remembers what it built and can modify it based on your feedback.

A perfectly valid workflow looks like this:

- 'Create a basic website for my pet-sitting business.'
- [AI creates something]
- 'Add a page listing my services and prices.'
- [AI adds it]
- 'Add a contact form that asks for pet type, dates needed, and any special care requirements.'
- [AI adds it]

- 'Change the color scheme to greens and browns—more natural and earthy.'
- [AI changes it]
- 'Add a section for testimonials from happy customers.'
- [AI adds it]
- 'The font is too small on mobile—make all text at least 16 pixels.'
- [AI fixes it]

Each step builds on the last. You don't need to describe everything upfront in a massive prompt. This iterative approach is actually how most people vibe code in practice. Start with the core, see what you get, refine.

That said, a more detailed initial prompt usually means fewer iterations needed. It's a tradeoff between upfront effort and iteration time. For simple projects, quick prompts work fine. For complex projects, investing more in the initial prompt pays off.

Common Prompt Mistakes (And How to Fix Them)

Let me share the mistakes I see most often, so you can avoid them:

Mistake 1: Being Too Vague

"Make it better."

Better how? This tells the AI nothing. It will make random changes that may or may not be improvements from your perspective.

"The text is too small for older users. Increase all body text to at least 16 pixels and add more white space between paragraphs so it's easier to read."

Now the AI knows exactly what to change and why.

Mistake 2: Assuming the AI Knows Context

"Add a standard checkout process."

There's no single 'standard' checkout. Different industries, different products, different customer expectations. The AI will guess, and it might guess wrong.

> "Add a checkout process with these steps: (1) shopping cart review where customers can change quantities or remove items, (2) shipping address entry with validation, (3) payment with credit card through Stripe including fields for card number, expiration, and CVV, (4) order confirmation page that shows what they ordered and sends an email receipt."

Explicit is always better than implicit.

Mistake 3: Forgetting Mobile Users

> "Create a dashboard showing our sales data."

Will this dashboard be used on phones? Tablets? Desktop computers? All of the above? The design should be different for each.

> "Create a dashboard showing our sales data. It needs to work well on both desktop computers and mobile phones. On desktop, show charts side by side. On mobile, stack them vertically so they're still readable. Make sure touch targets are big enough for fingers, not just mouse cursors."

Mistake 4: Describing Solutions Instead of Problems

> "Add a red banner at the top of the page using JavaScript that can be dismissed when clicked."

You're prescribing a specific technical solution. The AI will implement exactly what you asked for, even if there's a better approach.

> "I need a way to show urgent announcements to all users as soon as they visit the site. The announcement should be prominent but not block the whole page, and users should be able to dismiss it so it doesn't keep bothering them."

When you describe the problem instead of a specific solution, you let the AI suggest approaches you might not have thought of. Often it knows better ways to accomplish what you need.

Mistake 5: Writing a Novel

Yes, I said to be detailed—but there's a balance. If your prompt is 2,000 words of rambling thoughts, the AI may struggle to identify what's actually important. Be thorough but organized. Use bullet points for lists of features. Group related ideas together.

The Iteration Mindset

The biggest mindset shift in vibe coding is accepting that iteration is normal, not failure.

Professional developers iterate constantly. They write something, test it, find problems, fix them, test again, improve it. This isn't a sign that they don't know what they're doing—it's how software development works. Nobody gets everything perfect on the first try, not even experts.

When your first prompt doesn't produce exactly what you want, that's fine. It's expected. Just describe what needs to change and keep going.

> *"The contact form is good, but I also need a field for their preferred contact method—phone or email—and a checkbox where they consent to receiving occasional updates from us. Make the submit button more prominent too; it's getting lost."*

Each iteration gets you closer to what you want. Usually, three to five rounds of refinement will get you something you're happy with. Complex projects might take ten to twenty rounds, and that's still dramatically faster than the old way of building software.

Tip

Keep track of what works. When you write a prompt that produces great results, save it somewhere. Over time, you'll build a personal library of effective prompts that you can adapt for future projects.

Practice Time: Your First Real Prompt

Before we move to actual building in the next chapter, let's practice writing a prompt. Think of something simple you'd like to create—maybe:

- A personal website showcasing your work or hobbies
- A shared to-do list for your family
- A sign-up form for an upcoming event you're organizing
- A simple tracking tool for a habit you want to build
- A directory of contacts for a group you're part of

Now write a prompt for it using the formula:

Your Template

I want to build [WHAT] for [WHO] because [WHY]. It needs to [FEATURES]. The look should be [AESTHETIC].

Write it down somewhere—in a notes app, in this book's margins, wherever works for you. Make it specific. Include details. Describe the vibe.

In the next chapter, you'll actually use this prompt (or something like it) to build your first real project. The skills you've learned here—specificity, user focus, purpose, features, aesthetic—will guide everything you build from now on.

4 Your First Build

From Zero to Website in 30 Minutes

Enough theory. Let's build something real.

In this chapter, you'll create your first project—a personal website. By the end, you'll have something live on the internet that you can share with anyone in the world. Not a mockup. Not a prototype. A real, working website with your name on it.

This isn't just an exercise. The website you build today can be your actual online presence if you want it to be. Or it can be practice for the more complex projects ahead. Either way, you're about to prove to yourself that this vibe coding thing actually works.

Ready? Let's go.

Step 1: Open Lovable

Go to lovable.dev and sign in with the account you created earlier. If you haven't created an account yet, do it now—it only takes a minute, and you can use your Google account to sign up quickly.

When you land on the dashboard, you'll see a text box asking what you want to build. It might say something like 'What do you want to create?' or 'Describe your app.' This simple text box is your gateway to creating real software.

Take a moment to appreciate what's happening here. A few years ago, this text box would have been a code editor requiring years of training to use. Now it speaks English.

Step 2: Describe Your Website

Type a description of what you want. Here's an example you can use as a starting point, but I strongly encourage you to modify it with your own real details:

> **Sample Prompt**
>
> Create a personal website for me. My name is [YOUR NAME] and I'm a [YOUR PROFESSION/ROLE]. Include an About Me section with a brief bio explaining who I am and what I'm passionate about. Add a section highlighting my skills, experience, or what I do for work. Include a section for my interests or hobbies outside of work. Finally, add a contact section with my email address and links to my social media profiles. Use a clean, modern design with a warm color palette—maybe soft blues and warm grays. Make it friendly and approachable, not cold or corporate. It should work well on both phones and computers.

Replace the bracketed parts with your real information. Feel free to add, remove, or change sections based on what you actually want. Some ideas:

- If you're a freelancer, add a portfolio section
- If you're job hunting, emphasize your professional experience
- If this is more personal, focus on hobbies and interests
- If you want to be contacted, add a contact form instead of just email

The prompt doesn't have to be perfect. Remember what we learned in the last chapter—we can iterate and improve. But put in some real details; the more specific you are, the better your first version will be.

Once you're happy with your prompt, hit Enter or click the button to submit.

Step 3: Watch the Magic Happen

Lovable will now generate your website. You'll see it working—thinking about your request, creating components, writing code, assembling your site. This usually takes 30 seconds to a minute.

Watch the process. It's fascinating to see the AI interpret your words and turn them into a real design. You might see it create a header first, then build out sections, then add styling. The exact process varies, but the result is the same: a working website built from your description.

When it's done, you'll see a preview of your website right in the browser. You can click around in the preview to test it. Scroll through the page. Click any links or buttons. See what it created.

Take a moment to actually look at it. Not just a glance—really look. Read the text. Notice the colors. See how the layout works. Check it on mobile view if there's a toggle for that.

Pretty cool, right? You just created a website by describing what you wanted in English.

Step 4: Make It Yours Through Iteration

It's rare that the first version is exactly perfect. That's completely fine—now we iterate. This is where vibe coding really shines: you can refine your creation through conversation.

Look at your site critically and think about what you'd change. Then describe those changes in the chat. The AI remembers what it built and can modify it based on your feedback.

Here are some example refinements you might make:

"The header looks good, but I'd like my name to be bigger and more prominent. Make it the first thing people notice."

"Add a photo section where I can showcase some pictures of my work. Create a grid layout that looks good with 6-12 images."

"Change the main color from blue to a sage green. Keep the overall color scheme harmonious but use green as the primary accent."

"The font is a bit formal for my personality. Switch to something more friendly and approachable."

"Add my LinkedIn and Instagram links with icons in the contact section. Use recognizable icons that people will understand."

"The text is a bit small on my phone. Make all body text at least 16 pixels so it's easier to read without zooming."

"Add more white space between sections—it feels a little cramped. Let the design breathe more."

"The About Me section feels too long. Break it into shorter paragraphs and add a subtle background color to make it more readable."

Each change builds on what's already there. You don't have to start over. The AI remembers the context and modifies the existing site.

Make three or four changes. Watch how the AI responds to each one. Notice how it preserves what you liked while changing what you asked for. This back-and-forth is the essence of vibe coding.

Step 5: Go Live

Once you're happy with your site—or at least happy enough for now—it's time to put it on the internet for real.

In Lovable, look for the 'Deploy' or 'Publish' button (the exact label may vary depending on when you're reading this, but it's usually prominent and obvious). Click it and follow the prompts.

The platform will handle all the technical stuff: setting up hosting, configuring the domain, making sure everything works. Within moments, your website will be live with a URL you can share—something like yourname.lovable.app or similar.

That's it. You built a website. It's real. It's live. It's on the internet.

Copy that URL. Text it to a friend. Email it to a family member. Post it on social media. You made this. Not a template you filled in—a custom website built to your specifications by describing what you wanted.

What Just Happened: Understanding the Miracle

Let's pause and appreciate what you just did, because it's easy to take for granted:

You wrote a few sentences in English—the same language you use to text friends or write emails. The AI translated those sentences into code—HTML for structure, CSS for styling, JavaScript for interactivity. It assembled that code into a working website. It deployed that website to a server somewhere in the world. And it gave you a link to share with anyone.

A few years ago, doing all of that would require:

- Learning web development: HTML, CSS, JavaScript—months of study minimum
- Writing the code yourself: days or weeks of actual work for something this polished
- Setting up hosting: researching options, configuring servers, hours of confusion
- Configuring domains and SSL certificates: more technical details to learn
- Debugging why it doesn't work on some browsers: frustration and Stack Overflow
- Making it look good on mobile: responsive design is a skill unto itself

You did it in 30 minutes with no prior experience. The playing field has fundamentally changed.

> This is the power of vibe coding. This is why I wrote this book. This is why everything has changed for people with ideas but without technical backgrounds.

Troubleshooting Common Issues

Sometimes things don't go perfectly. Here's how to handle common situations:

"It doesn't look like what I imagined"

This is the most common issue, and it's totally normal. The AI can't read your mind—it can only interpret your words. The solution is to describe specifically what's different from your vision.

Don't say 'it's wrong' or 'I don't like it.' Instead, be specific: 'I wanted more white space between sections' or 'The photo should be on the left side, not the top' or 'The colors are too bright; I wanted something more muted and professional.'

The more specific your feedback, the better the AI can adjust.

"It made something completely different from what I asked for"

Your prompt might have been too vague or ambiguous. Try being more specific in your follow-up. Instead of just repeating your original request, add more details.

You can also try rephrasing entirely. Sometimes a different way of describing the same thing produces better results. If 'portfolio site' didn't work well, try 'a website showcasing my photography work with a grid of images.'

"It keeps changing things I already liked"

Be explicit about what to preserve: 'Keep the header exactly as it is, but change only the footer to include social media links' or 'Don't change anything about the color scheme—just modify the contact form to add a phone number field.'

When you specifically call out what should stay the same, the AI is much better at making targeted changes.

"I don't see a deploy button"

Different platforms have different interfaces, and they update frequently. Look for words like 'Deploy,' 'Publish,' 'Share,' 'Go Live,' or 'Launch.' Check the top-right corner of the screen, any menu options, or the sidebar. If you're truly stuck, type in the chat: 'How do I deploy this site?' The AI assistant can guide you through the current interface.

"Something broke that was working before"

Most platforms have version history or undo features. Look for a way to go back to a previous version. In Lovable, you can often see past versions and restore them. If you can't find it, ask the AI: 'Something broke. Can you undo the last change?' or 'Go back to how the site looked before the last modification.'

"It's taking forever to load"

Complex requests take longer to process. If it's been more than a minute or two, there might be an issue. Try refreshing the page and submitting your request again. If it happens repeatedly, try simplifying your request into smaller pieces.

Customization Ideas

Before moving on, I want you to make your website genuinely yours—not just an exercise. Here are some ideas for personalization:

- Your actual bio — Write who you really are, not placeholder text. What do you do? What are you passionate about? What would you want a stranger to know about you?
- Real projects or work — Add examples of things you've actually done. Even if they're small, they're real and they're yours.
- Authentic interests — Share your real hobbies and interests. These make you human and relatable.
- Contact information you'll actually check — Don't add a contact form that goes to an email you never open. Make it useful.
- Something unexpected — A favorite quote. Your current reading list. A hobby collection. Photos from a recent trip. Something that's uniquely you.

This is your space on the internet. Make it yours.

Homework: Share and Reflect

Before you move on to the next chapter, do two things:

1. Share your website with at least one real person. Text the link to a friend or family member. See their reaction. Ask them what they think. This is your creation, and it deserves an audience—even a small one.

2. Reflect on what you just did. You built a website by describing what you wanted. Think about what else you could build with this skill. What problems could you solve? What ideas could you bring to life?

In the next chapter, we're going to build something more complex—an application that actually does things, not just displays information. The skills you learned here transfer directly. The prompting, the iteration, the refinement—it all works the same way, just with more features to describe.

5 Building a Web App That Solves a Problem

From Website to Application

A website displays information. An application does things—it takes input, processes it, saves data, and provides real functionality that makes people's lives easier. In this chapter, we're building something that actually works, something that solves a real problem in the real world.

The line between website and app can be blurry, but here's a simple way to think about it: if users just read or look at it, it's a website. If they interact with it meaningfully, create things, save data, or rely on it to function day-to-day, it's an application.

Your personal website from Chapter 4 was a great start. Now we're going to build something that does more—something that could genuinely improve how you, your organization, or your community operates.

What Makes a Good First App Project

Not every idea makes a good first project. Here's what to look for:

- A real problem you understand well. The best apps solve problems you've personally experienced. You understand the frustrations, the edge cases, the ways current solutions fall short.
- Something simple at its core. Even if you have grand visions, the core functionality should be describable in a sentence or two. 'People sign up for time slots.' 'Users track their daily habits.' 'Customers submit requests and get quotes.'
- A clear user base. Who will use this? Even if it's just you and a few friends, that's fine. Having real users in

mind helps you make better decisions.

- Something you'll actually use. The best feedback comes from using your own creation. If you build something you don't need, you'll miss obvious problems.

Project Ideas by Category

Let me give you concrete ideas across different areas of life. Pick one that resonates with you, or let these inspire something specific to your situation.

For Teachers and Educators:

- Classroom Supply Tracker — Log what supplies you have, what's running low, what you've loaned to students. Never run out of glue sticks during an art project again.
- Parent Volunteer Coordinator — Post opportunities, let parents sign up, send reminders, track participation. Replace those paper sign-up sheets.
- Student Reading Log — Students log books they've read with brief reflections. You see class progress at a glance and can celebrate milestones.
- Assignment Submission Portal — Students submit work, you track what's in and what's missing, parents can check status.
- Seating Chart Manager — Create different arrangements, try them out, save configurations that work well for different activities.
- Field Trip Organizer — Permission slips, chaperone sign-ups, group assignments, emergency contacts all in one place.

For Small Business Owners:

- Appointment Scheduler — Let customers book their own appointments, reduce phone calls, send automatic reminders.
- Simple Inventory Tracker — Know what's in stock, get alerts when items are low, track what sells fastest.

• Customer Feedback Collector — Gather reviews and suggestions in one place, respond to concerns, spot patterns.

• Service Quote Calculator — Customers answer questions, get instant estimates. Saves time on routine inquiries.

• Client Contact Manager — Track customer history, preferences, past purchases, follow-up dates.

• Invoice Generator — Create professional invoices quickly, track what's paid and what's outstanding.

For Community Organizations:

• Volunteer Shift Scheduler — Post available shifts, let volunteers claim them, send reminders, track hours.

• Event Sign-Up System — Registration, waitlists, payments if needed, automatic confirmations.

• Meal Train Coordinator — When someone needs meals (new baby, illness, loss), coordinate who's bringing what when.

• Resource Lending Library — Track items that get borrowed and returned—tools, equipment, books.

• Prayer Request Board — Submit requests, see community needs, track answers and updates.

• Committee Task Tracker — Who's doing what, deadlines, status updates, meeting notes.

For Personal Life:

• Habit Tracker with Streaks — Track daily habits, see your streaks, get encouragement to keep going.

• Family Chore Rotator — Fair distribution of household tasks, automatic rotation, tracking completion.

• Shared Grocery List — Family members add items, anyone can check things off while shopping.

• Recipe Keeper with Meal Planning — Save recipes, plan weekly meals, generate shopping lists.

• Budget Tracker — Log expenses, categorize spending, see where your money goes.

- Gift Idea Notebook — Record gift ideas for people as you think of them, never forget before birthdays.

Building Your App: The Complete Process

Let's walk through building a real app from start to finish. I'll use a volunteer scheduler for a food bank as our example, but the process applies to any project.

Step 1: Define the Problem Clearly

Before writing any prompt, get crystal clear on what you're solving. Write it down:

Our food bank relies on volunteers for everything—sorting donations, stocking shelves, helping clients. Right now, the volunteer coordinator manages everything through email and a spreadsheet. It's a mess. Shifts get double-booked. People forget they signed up and don't show. The coordinator spends hours every week just managing the schedule instead of doing more valuable work. We need a better system.

Notice how specific this is. It's not 'we need volunteer software.' It's a detailed description of the actual problem, the current solution's failures, and the real impact.

Step 2: Identify the Users and Their Needs

Who will use this app? What does each type of user need?

Volunteers:

- See available shifts without back-and-forth emails
- Sign up easily from their phone
- Get reminders so they don't forget
- Cancel if something comes up (life happens)
- See their own history and upcoming commitments

Coordinators:

- Create and manage shifts without spreadsheet gymnastics
- See at a glance who's signed up for what
- Know immediately when shifts are understaffed
- Communicate with volunteers easily
- Get data for reporting and grant applications

Step 3: Write Your Initial Prompt

Now combine everything into a comprehensive prompt:

Complete App Prompt

Build a volunteer scheduling system for our community food bank. Currently everything is managed through email and spreadsheets, which leads to double-bookings, forgotten shifts, and hours of administrative work. The system needs two types of users: VOLUNTEERS should be able to: - See available shifts for the next 2 weeks - Sign up for shifts with one click - Get automatic email reminders 24 hours before their shift - Cancel a shift (which frees the spot for someone else) - See their own signup history and upcoming shifts COORDINATORS should be able to: - Create new shifts with date, time, location, and number of volunteers needed - Edit or delete shifts - See who's signed up for each shift - Get alerts when shifts are understaffed (less than 48 hours away with open spots) - Send messages to all volunteers signed up for a specific shift - Export the schedule to print or share The design should feel warm and welcoming—volunteers are donating their time, so we want them to feel appreciated, not processed. Use friendly colors, nothing cold or corporate. The app must work well on phones since most volunteers will access it that way.

Step 4: Submit and Observe

Paste this prompt into Lovable and submit. Watch what happens. The AI will create:

- A database structure to store shifts, users, and signups
- User authentication so volunteers can have accounts
- The volunteer-facing interface with shift listings

- The coordinator dashboard with management tools
- Email notification functionality
- A responsive design that works on phones and computers

This initial generation usually takes 60-90 seconds for a complex app like this. Don't worry if it's not perfect—that's what iteration is for.

Step 5: Test Everything

Before making changes, actually use what was built:

- Create a test coordinator account
- Create a few shifts
- Create a test volunteer account (use a different email or browser)
- Sign up for a shift as the volunteer
- Check if the signup appears in the coordinator view
- Cancel the signup
- Try edge cases: What happens if all spots are taken? What if you sign up twice?

Take notes on what works, what doesn't, and what's missing.

Iteration: Making It Better

Your first version won't be perfect. Here's how to improve it through conversation:

Adding Missing Features:

"Add a way for coordinators to create recurring shifts. If we have 'Food Sorting' every Tuesday from 9-12, I don't want to create it manually each week. Let me set it up once and have it repeat."

"Add a simple report showing total volunteer hours per month, broken down by volunteer. We need this for grant applications."

"Let volunteers set their availability preferences—which days/times they're generally available—so they only see shifts

that match."

Fixing Issues:

"The shift cards on mobile are too cramped. Add more spacing between them so they're easier to tap without accidentally hitting the wrong one."

"When I sign up for a shift and refresh the page, the signup confirmation message disappears but so does any indication that I'm signed up. Show a 'You're signed up!' badge on shifts I've claimed."

"The email reminders aren't sending. Can you check the email configuration and make sure it's set up correctly?"

Improving the Experience:

"Add a thank-you message that appears after volunteers complete a shift, telling them how much we appreciate their help and showing their total contribution hours."

"The coordinator dashboard is overwhelming. Organize it with tabs: 'Upcoming Shifts' as the default view, 'Past Shifts' for history, and 'Reports' for data."

Important

Make changes one at a time and test after each one. If you request five changes at once and something breaks, you won't know which change caused the problem.

Common Features and How to Request Them

Here are features you might want in various apps, with example prompts:

User Accounts and Login:

"Add user accounts. People should sign up with their email and create a password. Send a verification email before they can access everything."

Different User Roles:

"Create two types of users: regular users and admins. Admins can see everything and manage users. Regular users only see their own stuff."

Email Notifications:

"Send an email notification when someone submits a new request. Include the details of the request in the email."

Search and Filtering:

"Add a search bar that filters the list as you type. Also add dropdown filters for status, date range, and category."

File Uploads:

"Let users upload images when they submit an entry. Accept jpg, png, and gif. Show thumbnails in the list view."

Data Export:

"Add a button that exports all the data to a CSV file that opens in Excel."

Mobile Responsiveness:

"Make sure this works well on phones. The sidebar should become a hamburger menu, and the table should scroll horizontally on small screens."

Testing Like a Real User

Before sharing your app with real users, test it thoroughly:

- Happy path testing: Go through the normal flow like a regular user would. Sign up, use features, complete tasks. Does everything work smoothly?
- Edge case testing: Try unusual situations. Empty forms, very long text, special characters, clicking buttons multiple times quickly. What breaks?
- Mobile testing: Use your actual phone, not just the browser's mobile preview. Tap targets, scrolling, keyboard behavior—these often feel different on real devices.

- Multiple browsers: Try Chrome, Safari, Firefox if possible. Some things work in one browser but not another.
- Fresh eyes testing: Have someone who doesn't know the app try to use it without any instructions. Watch where they get confused.

> **Tip**
> When testing reveals problems, describe them specifically. 'When I submit the form with only spaces in the name field, it accepts it but then the name shows as blank on the list' is much more helpful than 'forms are buggy.'

Deploying and Sharing

Once your app works well, it's time to share it with real users.

Soft Launch: Start with a small group—maybe 5-10 people who will be patient and give honest feedback. Tell them it's a test version. This is your chance to catch issues before wider release.

Gather Feedback: Make it easy for early users to report problems and suggestions. A simple feedback form or even a shared document works. Ask specific questions: What confused you? What's missing? What do you like?

Iterate Based on Feedback: Real users will find issues you missed and want features you didn't think of. This feedback is gold. Prioritize fixes for things that block people from using the app, then add the most-requested features.

Gradual Rollout: Once your soft launch users are happy, expand slowly. Double your user base, stabilize, then double again. This prevents being overwhelmed by support requests and gives you time to fix issues that only appear at scale.

Your Assignment

Before moving to the next chapter, build an app that solves a real problem in your life. Not a toy project—something you'll actually use.

- Pick a problem from the ideas earlier, or identify your own
- Define the users and their needs
- Write a comprehensive prompt using the template
- Build it, test it, iterate until it works
- Deploy it and start using it for real

When you've used your own app for a week, you'll have learned more about vibe coding than any tutorial could teach. The experience of building something real, encountering problems, solving them, and seeing people (even if that's just you) use your creation—that's where the learning really happens.

6 Building a Mobile App

Apps That Live on Your Phone

There's something special about a mobile app. Something with its own icon on your home screen. Something that feels native to your device, that you can tap to open without navigating to a website. In this chapter, you'll build one.

Mobile apps have a different feel than web apps. They're more personal—they live on the device you carry everywhere. They can send you notifications, access your camera, know your location (with permission). They feel more integrated into your life.

The good news: building mobile apps has gotten dramatically easier with vibe coding tools. You don't need to learn Swift or Kotlin or deal with the complexity of app development. You can describe what you want and get a native app.

Web Apps vs. Native Mobile Apps

Before we build, let's understand the difference:

Web App (Progressive Web App / PWA):

- Runs in a browser (Chrome, Safari)
- You visit a URL to access it
- Can be 'installed' as a shortcut on your home screen
- Works on any device with a modern browser
- Limited access to device features
- Easier to build and update

Native Mobile App:

- Downloaded from the App Store or Google Play Store
- Has its own icon that looks like any other app

- Can access device features: camera, push notifications, GPS, contacts, health data
- Feels more integrated with the phone's operating system
- Users expect a certain level of polish and reliability
- Requires approval from Apple/Google to publish

Web apps are easier to build, easier to update, and easier to share (just send a link). Native apps feel more 'real,' can do more things, and benefit from app store discovery. The right choice depends on your specific project and users.

> **Tip**
>
> If your app doesn't need push notifications, camera access, or other device features—and if your users will access it from different devices—a web app might be the better choice. If you need device integration or want that 'real app' experience, go native.

Using CreateAnything

CreateAnything (formerly Create.xyz) is built specifically for creating native mobile apps through vibe coding. Go to createanything.com and sign in.

The interface is similar to other vibe coding tools—a chat where you describe what you want. The key difference is what happens behind the scenes: CreateAnything generates native iOS and Android apps, not web apps.

Features that make CreateAnything special:

- Native app generation — Real apps that can be published to app stores, not just web wrappers
- Live preview on your phone — Scan a QR code and see your app on your actual device as you build
- Built-in backend — Database, user authentication, and API all included
- One-click App Store submission — Streamlined process for publishing

- Self-correcting AI — The system detects and fixes many errors automatically

Your First Mobile App: A Habit Tracker

Let's build something you'll actually use every day—a habit tracker. The goal is to help you build and maintain positive habits by tracking streaks and visualizing progress.

> **Habit Tracker Prompt**
>
> Create a daily habit tracking app for my personal use. I want to track three habits: drinking enough water (8 glasses), exercising for at least 30 minutes, and reading for at least 20 minutes. Features: - Each day, I see my three habits with a simple tap-to-complete button for each - When I complete a habit, the button changes to show a checkmark and celebrates briefly (maybe a subtle animation) - Show my current streak for each habit—how many consecutive days I've completed it - Show a weekly view so I can see patterns (maybe Sunday-Saturday as columns) - Include gentle reminder notifications that I can customize—what time, which habits - Let me see my history going back 30 days - Add the ability to add new habits or modify existing ones later Design should be calm and minimalist—soft colors, nothing harsh or clinical. This is about building positive habits, so it should feel encouraging, not judgmental. Make tapping the completion buttons feel satisfying.

Submit this and watch CreateAnything build your app. You'll see it generate the structure, design the interface, and set up the data storage. When it's ready, you can scan a QR code to see it running on your actual phone.

Test it out. Tap the completion buttons. Do they feel satisfying? Is the streak display clear? Try setting a reminder and see if it comes through. Make notes on what you'd improve.

Mobile-Specific Features

Mobile apps can do things web apps can't. Here's how to request common mobile features:

Push Notifications:

Push notifications appear even when the app isn't open—they're powerful for reminders and engagement.

> *"Add push notification reminders. Let me set a daily reminder time for each habit. The notification should say something encouraging like 'Time to drink water! You're on a 5-day streak—keep it going!'"*

> *"Send me a notification at 8pm if I haven't completed all my habits for the day. Frame it positively: 'Almost there! You've still got time to complete your reading habit.'"*

Camera Access:

Native apps can use your phone's camera for photos and video.

> *"Let me take a photo to log with my workout. I want to track my progress visually."*

> *"Add a feature to scan barcodes of the books I read and automatically pull in the title and author."*

Location Services:

With permission, apps can know where you are.

> *"Track the location where I complete habits—I'm curious if I'm better about exercising at the gym versus at home."*

> *"Remind me about my water habit when I arrive at work, since that's when I tend to forget."*

Health Data Integration (iOS):

iOS apps can read and write to Apple Health with user permission.

> *"Connect to Apple Health and automatically mark my exercise habit complete if Health shows at least 30 minutes of workout activity."*

Widgets:

Home screen widgets let users see information without opening the app.

> *"Create a home screen widget showing today's habit completion status—three circles that fill in as I complete each habit."*

Offline Mode:

Let the app work without internet and sync when connected.

> *"Make sure the app works offline. I want to log habits even if I don't have cell service. Sync everything when I get back online."*

Iterating on Your Mobile App

Just like with web apps, iteration is key. Use your app for a few days, then make improvements:

> *"The completion buttons are too small—I keep missing them. Make them bigger and add more padding around them."*

> *"I want to add a new habit: 'No social media before noon.' Add a way for me to create custom habits with custom names."*

> *"The weekly view is confusing. Make today's column highlighted and add labels for which day is which."*

> *"Add a small celebration animation when I complete all habits for the day—something satisfying but not over the top."*

> *"I want to share my streak screenshots with friends. Add a 'Share' button that creates a nice-looking image of my current streaks."*

Publishing to the App Store

If you want your app available for anyone to download, you'll need to publish it to Apple's App Store (for iPhones) or Google Play (for Android). CreateAnything helps streamline this process.

Requirements for Apple App Store:

• Apple Developer Account: $99/year. This is required for any iOS app publishing. Sign up at developer.apple.com.

• App Store Guidelines Compliance: Apple has rules about what apps can do, how they handle data, what content they contain. Most productivity apps comply easily, but review the guidelines.

• App Review: Apple reviews every app before it goes live. This usually takes 1-3 days. They check for crashes, guideline compliance, and basic quality.

• App Metadata: You'll need a description, screenshots, keywords, privacy policy, and other information.

Requirements for Google Play:

• Google Developer Account: One-time $25 fee. Sign up at play.google.com/console.

• Play Store Policies: Similar to Apple, but different in specifics. Generally easier to get approved.

• Review Process: Faster than Apple, often same-day.

Tip

If you're building something just for yourself, family, or a small group, you might not need app store publishing at all. iOS has TestFlight which lets you share your app with up to 100 people for testing without going through full review. Android lets you sideload apps directly.

When to Build Mobile vs. Web

Here's a framework for deciding:

Build a native mobile app when:

• You need push notifications that work reliably
• You need camera, GPS, or other device hardware
• The app is for personal daily use (like a habit tracker)
• You want presence on app stores for discovery

• Your users primarily use phones and expect a native experience

Build a web app when:

• Users need to access from multiple devices (phone, computer, tablet)
• You need to update frequently without app store review delays
• Your users aren't technical enough to download apps
• You want the simplest possible sharing (just send a link)
• The app is for occasional use, not daily habits

Build both when:

• You have resources for both and users on all platforms
• You want maximum reach and optimal experience everywhere
• The core features work well on both but you want device integration on mobile

Your Assignment

Build a mobile app you'll actually use daily. Some ideas beyond habit trackers:

• Mood Journal: Log your mood a few times a day, see patterns over time
• Gratitude Log: Record three things you're grateful for each day
• Water Tracker: Simple, focused on just water intake with reminder notifications
• Workout Timer: Customizable interval timers for your exercise routine
• Daily Questions: Prompts that help you reflect on your day

The key is to build something you'll open every day. Use it for a full week before deciding it's 'done.' Living with your own app reveals improvements you'd never think of otherwise.

7 Building Something You Can Sell

From Hobby to Income

You've built websites, web apps, and mobile apps for yourself and your community. Now let's talk about building something that generates income—something people might actually pay for.

This is called SaaS—Software as a Service. Instead of selling a product once, you provide ongoing value and charge a subscription. Think of Netflix for movies, Spotify for music, or Dropbox for storage. Users pay monthly or yearly for continued access to software that runs in the cloud.

The SaaS model is powerful because it creates recurring revenue. Instead of constantly finding new customers, you build relationships with existing ones who pay you month after month. Even a small, niche product can generate meaningful income.

And here's the exciting part: You can build a SaaS product with vibe coding. The same skills you've been developing—clear communication, iterative building, understanding user needs—apply directly to building products people will pay for.

The Mindset Shift

Building for yourself is different from building for paying customers. When it's just you, imperfections are tolerable. When people are paying, expectations are higher.

Here's what changes:

- You must solve a real problem. Not a problem you think people should have—a problem they actually experience and would pay to solve. This requires research, not assumptions.

• You must solve it better. People already have solutions, even if those solutions are clunky spreadsheets or manual processes. Your tool needs to be meaningfully better to justify switching.

• You must make switching easy. The friction of trying something new is real. Your app needs to be simple enough that someone can start using it and see value quickly.

• You must price appropriately. Too high and people won't try it. Too low and they won't take it seriously (or you won't make enough to sustain the business).

• You must keep providing value. Subscriptions require ongoing relationships. If your customers don't keep getting value, they'll cancel.

Finding Your Niche

The biggest mistake new SaaS builders make: going too broad.

> **Important**
>
> Don't try to build 'a project management tool.' There are literally thousands of those—Asana, Monday, Basecamp, ClickUp, Notion, and on and on. You'll never compete with their features, their marketing budgets, their established user bases. You'll exhaust yourself trying to be everything for everyone.

Instead, go narrow. Incredibly narrow. Build 'a project management tool for wedding photographers' or 'a client scheduler for mobile dog groomers' or 'a inventory tracker for food truck owners.'

Why niches work:

• Less competition. Big companies ignore small niches. There's no 'Salesforce for tattoo shops' because the market is too small for them to care. That's your opportunity.

• Easier marketing. You know exactly who to reach and where they hang out. Dog groomers have Facebook groups, trade magazines, conferences. You can find them.

• Better product. You can specialize in exactly their problems. General tools have features for everyone, which means features for no one in particular. Your tool can be perfect for your niche.

• Word of mouth. Niche communities talk to each other. One happy wedding photographer tells five other wedding photographers. In a niche, referrals spread fast.

• Premium pricing. A general tool competes on price with a hundred alternatives. A specialized tool can charge more because it fits better.

How do you find a good niche? Look for:

• Problems you understand firsthand. Your own profession, hobby, community.

• People who can afford to pay. Business tools sell better than consumer tools because businesses have budgets.

• Underserved markets. Groups using outdated software, spreadsheets, or paper.

• Passionate communities. People who identify strongly with their niche and want tools made specifically for them.

The MVP Approach

MVP stands for Minimum Viable Product. It's the smallest version of your idea that could actually work and provide value. Not a feature-complete product—the minimum needed to test whether your idea is worth pursuing.

Why start with an MVP?

• You don't know what users want. Really. Your assumptions about what matters are probably wrong in important ways. An MVP gets you real feedback fast.

• Time is precious. Building everything you imagine could take months. If the core idea doesn't work, you've wasted that time.

• Perfect is the enemy of shipped. You can polish forever. An imperfect product in users' hands teaches you more than a perfect product in your imagination.

Here's an example. Say you want to build a client management system for dog trainers:

Your full vision includes: client profiles, dog profiles, training history, progress tracking, automated appointment reminders, payment processing, multi-location support, employee management, detailed analytics, training plan templates, photo/video logging, integration with scheduling tools, customer portal, mobile app, and on and on...

Your MVP includes: client profiles with their dogs, ability to log training sessions with notes, and a calendar showing upcoming appointments.

That's it. The MVP is enough to be useful. A dog trainer could actually use it to track their clients and sessions. It solves a real problem, even if imperfectly.

Once real trainers are using it, you'll learn what they actually want next. Maybe they desperately need payment processing but don't care about templates. Maybe they want photo logging but multi-location doesn't matter to anyone. Real users tell you what to build next.

> **MVP Prompt Example**
> Build a simple client management system for independent dog trainers. Features: - Client list with name, email, phone, address - Each client can have multiple dogs with breed, age, and notes - Log training sessions with date, dog, duration, and freeform notes about what was covered - Simple calendar view showing scheduled sessions - Search clients by name or dog name Keep it simple and focused. Clean design, easy to use on both phone and computer. This is for solo trainers managing their own client base, not large training facilities.

Validating Before Building

Here's a secret that can save you months of wasted effort: Validate your idea before building it.

Validation means checking whether people actually want what you're planning to build—ideally whether they'll pay for it.

- Talk to potential users. Find 10 people in your target niche and have real conversations. What tools do they currently use? What frustrates them? What would they pay for a solution?
- Search for existing solutions. If nothing exists, ask why. Maybe there's no market. If things exist but are bad, that's an opportunity.
- Create a landing page. Describe your product before it exists. Collect email addresses of interested people. If nobody signs up, that's useful data.
- Pre-sell. Some people offer discounted 'founding member' access before the product is built. If people pay before seeing the product, you have real validation.

Validation isn't about being 100% sure. It's about reducing risk. Every conversation, every signup, every piece of feedback makes your eventual product better and your success more likely.

Adding Payment Processing

If you're going to charge money, your app needs payment processing. Stripe is the standard solution—it handles all the complexity of credit cards, subscriptions, receipts, and payouts.

Stripe Integration Prompt

Add subscription billing through Stripe. Pricing structure: - Free 14-day trial (no credit card required to start) - After trial: $29/month or $290/year (2 months free) - Users should be able to manage their subscription from account settings: upgrade, downgrade, update payment method, cancel Show a clear pricing page explaining what they get. After signup, show a notice about trial days remaining. Send an email 3 days before trial ends reminding them to subscribe. If they don't subscribe, downgrade to a limited free tier that shows basic info but disables core features.

Setting up Stripe:

- Create a Stripe account at stripe.com (free)
- Get your API keys from the Stripe dashboard
- Connect them to your app when the AI prompts you
- Use Stripe's test mode to try everything before going live
- When ready, switch to live mode and start accepting real payments

Stripe takes about 2.9% + 30¢ per transaction in the US. On a $29 subscription, that's about $1.14, leaving you with $27.86. Factor this into your pricing.

Pricing Strategy

Pricing is part art, part science, and most people get it wrong in the same way: they price too low.

Principles to consider:

- Anchor to value, not cost. Your price should reflect how much value you provide, not how much effort you put in or what it costs you to run. If you save a trainer 5 hours a week, what's that worth to them?
- Research competitors. What do similar tools charge? You don't have to match them, but know the landscape. Being 10x more expensive than alternatives requires being significantly better. Being 10x cheaper might signal low quality.
- Consider psychology. $29 feels much cheaper than $30. Annual discounts encourage commitment. Odd pricing ($27/month) can signal precision.
- Start somewhere. You can always adjust later. A wrong price that gets you customers teaches you more than perfect pricing with no customers.
- Consider tiers. Basic/Pro/Premium lets different customers self-select. Some want the cheapest option; others want the best. Let them choose.

Common SaaS price points:

- Hobby/personal tools: $5-15/month
- Professional individual tools: $15-50/month
- Small business tools: $50-200/month
- Team tools: $10-30/user/month

The Reality of SaaS

I want to be honest with you about what to expect:

Most products don't find a large audience. The internet is full of abandoned SaaS projects. Even good products fail because of bad timing, weak marketing, or pure bad luck. This is normal, not a reflection of you.

Success takes time. Most 'overnight successes' took years to actually happen. Expect 1-2 years of steady work before meaningful revenue, if it happens at all.

Marketing matters as much as product. The best product in the world fails if nobody knows about it. You'll spend as much time on marketing as on building. Probably more.

Customer support is real work. Real customers have real questions, problems, and complaints. This takes time and energy you might not expect.

Churn is constant. Even happy customers cancel sometimes—they switch jobs, close businesses, find alternatives. You need to constantly add new customers to maintain revenue.

But here's the flip side:

A small niche product with just 100 customers at $20/month generates $2,000/month in recurring revenue. That's $24,000/year from a 'small' success. And unlike a job, once it's built and running, much of that revenue continues without your constant presence.

Other upsides:

- You're building an asset. A profitable SaaS can be sold. People buy these businesses for multiples of annual revenue.

• You're learning valuable skills. Building products, understanding users, marketing, sales—these skills transfer to future projects and opportunities.

• Failure teaches too. Even if this product doesn't succeed, you'll understand the process for the next one. Many successful founders had multiple failed attempts first.

Your Assignment

You don't have to build a SaaS right now. But if you're curious, here's how to start:

• Identify three niches you could potentially serve. These should be groups you understand or have access to.

• Talk to five people in one of those niches. Ask about their biggest frustrations, what tools they use, what they wish existed.

• Identify one problem that multiple people mentioned and would pay to solve.

• Define an MVP — the smallest thing that could solve that problem.

• Build it using everything you've learned.

• Share it with the people you interviewed. Get feedback. Iterate.

Maybe it turns into something. Maybe it doesn't. Either way, you'll learn more than you would by reading another chapter.

8 Leveling Up Your Skills

Going Beyond the Basics

You've come a long way. You can build websites, web apps, and mobile apps. You understand how to write prompts that get results and how to iterate until something works.

But this is just the beginning. As you take on more ambitious projects, you'll want to deepen your understanding and expand your capabilities. This chapter shows you how to keep growing.

I want to be clear: Everything in this chapter is optional. You can build amazing things with what you already know. But if you're curious, if you want more control, if you're drawn to understanding how things work under the hood—here's your path forward.

Understanding What's Happening Under the Hood

You don't need to become a programmer. But having a basic understanding of key technical concepts makes you a more effective vibe coder. You'll communicate more precisely, debug problems faster, and understand what's possible.

HTML (HyperText Markup Language):

Think of HTML as the skeleton of web pages. It defines what elements exist and their hierarchy: headings, paragraphs, images, buttons, forms, lists. When you ask for 'a header with my name and a navigation menu,' the AI generates HTML to create those elements.

A simple example: <h1>Welcome</h1> creates a big heading that says 'Welcome.' The h1 tag tells the browser this is a main heading.

CSS (Cascading Style Sheets):

CSS controls how things look—the visual design layer. Colors, fonts, spacing, layout, animations. It's what makes a page beautiful (or ugly). When you ask for 'soft blue colors and more whitespace,' the AI writes CSS to achieve that.

A simple example: *color: blue;* makes text blue. *padding: 20px;* adds space inside an element.

JavaScript:

JavaScript makes things interactive. When you click a button and something happens—a form submits, content changes, an animation plays—that's JavaScript. It's the behavior layer.

This is the most complex of the three, but you don't need to write it. Just know that when something 'does stuff' on a webpage, JavaScript is probably involved.

Database:

A database stores information permanently. Without one, everything would disappear when you close the browser. User accounts, saved content, settings, history—all stored in a database. Common databases include PostgreSQL, MySQL, and MongoDB.

When you ask for 'user accounts that save their preferences,' the AI sets up database tables to store that information.

API (Application Programming Interface):

An API is how different software systems talk to each other. When your app sends email through SendGrid, processes payment through Stripe, or gets weather data from a weather service, it's using their APIs.

APIs are like contracts: 'If you send me this information in this format, I'll do this thing and send you back a response.' You don't need to know the details, but understanding that external services connect via APIs helps you ask for integrations.

Using Cursor for More Control

As projects get more complex, you might want more direct control over what's happening. Cursor is an AI-powered code editor that lets you work with code directly while still getting AI assistance.

With Cursor, you can:

- Open projects you built in Lovable or Replit and make direct edits
- See and understand the actual code that powers your apps
- Make small, precise changes yourself instead of describing them
- Work on larger, more complex projects with many files
- Learn how code works by reading what the AI generates

Getting started with Cursor:

- Download from cursor.com and install it
- Export a project from Lovable or clone one from Replit
- Open the project folder in Cursor
- Explore the files and folders—most web projects have similar structures
- Use Cursor's chat to ask questions about what you're seeing

Example conversations with Cursor:

"Explain what this file does in simple terms. I'm not a programmer."

> *"Where is the code that handles the contact form submission? I want to understand how it works."*
>
> *"What would I change to make the header taller? Show me exactly which line."*
>
> *"Can you modify this button to have rounded corners and a shadow when hovered?"*

Cursor is a bridge between pure vibe coding and traditional programming. You can use as much or as little code knowledge as you have, and the AI fills in the gaps.

Common Integrations and How to Add Them

Modern apps rarely stand alone—they connect to other services for additional functionality. Here are common integrations and how to request them:

Email (SendGrid, Resend, Postmark):

Send automated emails—welcome messages, notifications, password resets, confirmations.

> *"Set up email sending using SendGrid. Send a welcome email when users sign up, and a password reset email when requested. Include my logo in the email template."*

SMS Text Messages (Twilio):

Send text message notifications or reminders.

> *"Add SMS notifications through Twilio. Send a text reminder 24 hours before scheduled appointments. Keep messages short and include a link to manage the appointment."*

Payment Processing (Stripe):

Accept credit cards, manage subscriptions, handle invoices.

> *"Integrate Stripe for payments. Offer monthly and yearly subscription options. Handle failed payments gracefully and send dunning emails."*

AI Features (OpenAI, Anthropic):

Add AI capabilities to your own apps—chatbots, content generation, analysis.

> *"Add an AI assistant that helps users write product descriptions. Users paste their rough notes, and the AI generates polished marketing copy. Use GPT-4 for quality."*

File Storage (AWS S3, Cloudinary):

Store uploaded files, images, documents in the cloud.

> *"Let users upload profile photos. Store images in Cloudinary and automatically resize them to standard dimensions. Show a default avatar if no photo is uploaded."*

Calendar Integration (Google Calendar):

Sync events with users' calendars.

> *"When a user schedules an appointment, create a Google Calendar event on their calendar (if they've connected their account) and on the admin's calendar."*

Analytics (PostHog, Mixpanel):

Track how users interact with your app.

> *"Add PostHog analytics. Track when users sign up, complete key actions, and upgrade to paid plans. I want to understand where users drop off."*

Each integration requires some setup—usually creating an account with the service and getting API keys. The AI will guide you through the process step by step.

Learning Resources (If You Want to Go Deeper)

Everything below is optional. You can be highly productive without any of it. But if you're curious:

Free coding fundamentals:

• FreeCodeCamp.org — Comprehensive free courses. Start with 'Responsive Web Design' for HTML/CSS basics.

- MDN Web Docs (developer.mozilla.org) — The authoritative reference for web technologies.
- Codecademy — Interactive lessons, some free.

Video learning:

- YouTube tutorials — Search 'HTML basics for beginners' or 'JavaScript crash course'
- Traversy Media — Clear, practical web development videos
- The Net Ninja — Extensive free tutorials

Tool-specific resources:

- Each tool's documentation — Lovable, Replit, CreateAnything all have help docs
- Official tutorials and examples
- Community forums and Discord servers

Books:

- 'HTML and CSS: Design and Build Websites' by Jon Duckett — Visual, beginner-friendly
- 'Don't Make Me Think' by Steve Krug — Classic on user experience design

Building Your Knowledge Over Time

You don't need to learn everything at once. A better approach:

- Learn just-in-time. When you encounter something you don't understand while building, learn about that specific thing. Context makes learning stick.
- Review AI output. When the AI generates code, occasionally ask it to explain what it created. You'll absorb concepts naturally over time.
- Try small experiments. Open your project in Cursor, find a simple style change, and try modifying the code yourself. See what happens.
- Be patient with yourself. Programming knowledge accumulates slowly. Don't expect to understand everything immediately.

Joining the Community

Vibe coding is better with others. You'll learn faster, stay motivated, and discover opportunities through community.

- Tool-specific communities: Lovable, Replit, and CreateAnything all have Discord servers or forums. Join them, lurk, and eventually ask questions.
- Reddit: r/nocode, r/webdev, r/learnprogramming, r/SideProject—communities for builders at various levels.
- Twitter/X: Follow builders who share their work. Search hashtags like #buildinpublic and #nocode. The energy is contagious.
- Local meetups: Search for entrepreneurship, maker, or tech meetups in your area. Even if you're not building startups, you'll meet people who understand what you're doing.
- Build in public: Share your progress online as you build. Screenshot your work, explain what you're creating, celebrate milestones. People are supportive, and you might find collaborators or early users.

Don't be intimidated by people who seem more advanced. Everyone started somewhere. Most communities are welcoming to genuine learners.

9 What Now?

You've Changed

When you started this book, you might have thought building apps was something other people did. Tech people. Programmers. People with computer science degrees.

Now you know better.

You've built a website, a web app, and learned to build mobile apps. You understand prompting, iteration, and deployment. You've joined the ranks of people who can turn ideas into reality.

> That's a fundamental shift in capability. The world looks different when you can build things.

Keep Building

The biggest danger now is that you stop. Skills fade without practice. Build something every month:

- A silly game for your kids
- A birthday countdown for someone you love
- A random quote generator with your favorite quotes
- A simple tool to solve a small daily annoyance
- An experiment with a feature you haven't tried

Small projects keep skills sharp and sometimes become bigger things.

Share What You Make

Building in isolation is less fun and less effective. Share your work:

- Show friends and family what you've created
- Post screenshots and links on social media

- Write about what you learned
- Help others just starting their journey

That scheduling tool for your food bank? Other food banks need it. That classroom app? Other teachers would love it. Put your work out there.

Teach Others

The best way to solidify learning is to teach. Find someone with ideas who thinks they can't build things. Show them this book. Sit with them as they build their first website.

The more people who can build, the more good software exists—software for nonprofits, communities, problems big tech ignores.

The Future

AI capabilities are improving rapidly. What's possible today will seem limited compared to next year. But the skills you've learned—clear communication, iteration, understanding users—remain valuable forever.

You're developing a way of thinking, not just learning tools.

A Final Thought

A few years ago, I had an idea—a scheduling app for my students. I thought I couldn't build it because I wasn't 'technical enough.'

I was wrong. The background I needed was describing what I wanted clearly. The skill I needed was patience to iterate. The tool I needed was AI that could translate my words into code.

I had all of that. I just didn't know it.

You have all of that too. You can text. You can describe what you want. You can say what you'd change. That's all you need.

Now go build something amazing.

Bonus: Real-World Success Stories

How Regular People Built Real Apps

Throughout this book, I've told you that vibe coding works. But don't just take my word for it. Here are real examples of non-programmers who built useful software.

The Teacher's Scheduling App

Sarah, a middle school math teacher in Ohio, was frustrated with how her school handled tutoring signups. Students who needed help couldn't easily find available time slots, and teachers spent hours coordinating schedules through email chains.

Using Lovable, Sarah built a tutoring scheduler in one weekend. Students see available slots, click to book, and get automatic reminders. Teachers set their availability and see who's coming. The app now handles over 200 tutoring sessions per month at her school.

Her prompt started simple: 'A tutoring signup system where students can see which teachers have open slots and book appointments.' She iterated from there, adding features as needs emerged.

The Church Volunteer Coordinator

Marcus ran volunteer coordination for his church's community meal program. Every week, he sent dozens of emails and texts trying to fill shifts. People would forget, double-book, or not respond. It was exhausting.

He built a volunteer management app that shows available shifts, lets people claim them with one tap, sends automatic reminders, and alerts him when shifts are understaffed. He went from spending 10 hours a week on coordination to about 1 hour.

The first version was rough. 'It looked terrible,' Marcus admits. But it worked. He improved the design over time based on volunteer feedback.

The Small Business Quote Calculator

Diana owns a small landscaping company. She was losing potential customers because quotes took too long—she had to visit properties, calculate materials, and manually create estimates. People often went with competitors who responded faster.

She built a quote calculator where customers answer questions about their property (size, current state, desired services) and get an instant estimate. It's not perfectly accurate, but it gives people a ballpark immediately and captures their information for follow-up.

Her close rate on leads from the calculator is nearly double her old rate from phone inquiries.

The Family Chore App

Jennifer, a mom of three teenagers, was tired of the 'I thought it was their turn' arguments about household chores. She built a simple chore rotation app that automatically assigns tasks weekly, tracks completion, and (this was the genius part) ties completion to wifi access.

'It's not sophisticated,' she says, 'but it ended 90% of our chore-related conflicts.' The app took her about three hours to build over two evenings.

Common Patterns in Success Stories

Looking at these and other success stories, patterns emerge:

- They solved their own problems first. Every successful builder started with something they personally needed. They understood the problem deeply because they lived it.

- They started simple. First versions were basic—sometimes embarrassingly so. Features came later, driven by real usage.

• They iterated based on feedback. Real users revealed issues and needs that the builders hadn't anticipated. The best apps evolved through use.

• They didn't wait for perfect. They shipped something usable and improved it over time. Progress over perfection.

• They stayed focused. Rather than building everything, they did one thing well. Focused tools outperform Swiss Army knives.

Bonus: Troubleshooting Guide

When Things Go Wrong

Things will go wrong. That's not a possibility—it's a certainty. Here's how to handle common problems.

Problem: The AI built something completely different from what I wanted

This usually means your prompt was too vague or ambiguous. The AI made reasonable assumptions that didn't match your mental picture.

Solutions:

- Be more specific in your follow-up. Don't just repeat the request—add details.

- Try rephrasing entirely. Sometimes different words get better results.

- Break your request into smaller pieces. Describe one feature at a time.

- Include examples of what you mean. 'Like Airbnb's search, but for...'

Problem: The design looks bad

AI-generated designs can be generic or mismatched to your vision.

Solutions:

- Describe the aesthetic more specifically: 'warm and friendly, like a coffee shop' vs 'clean and minimal, like Apple'

- Reference specific colors: 'Use soft sage green as the primary color'

- Request changes piece by piece: header, then content area, then footer

- Ask the AI to show you options: 'Give me three different color schemes to choose from'

Problem: A feature that was working suddenly broke
Changes can have unintended side effects.

Solutions:

- Look for version history or undo options in your tool
- Ask: 'The signup feature stopped working after the last change. Can you check what happened?'
- Be specific about what broke: 'Users can't submit the form—clicking the button does nothing'
- Test after each change, not after many changes bundled together

Problem: The app works on desktop but not on mobile
Responsive design (working across screen sizes) isn't automatic.

Solutions:

- Explicitly request mobile support: 'This must work well on phones'
- Test on your actual phone, not just browser resize
- Describe mobile-specific behavior: 'On mobile, stack these side-by-side elements vertically'

Problem: Users are confused by my app
What's obvious to you (the builder) isn't obvious to users.

Solutions:

- Watch someone use your app without helping them
- Add labels, instructions, and placeholder text
- Simplify—remove features users don't need
- Ask: 'Add a brief onboarding flow explaining how to use the main features'

Problem: The app is slow
Performance issues can frustrate users.

Solutions:

- Ask the AI to optimize: 'The list is loading slowly with 1000+ items. Can you add pagination or virtual scrolling?'
- Reduce image sizes
- Load data on demand instead of all at once

Getting Unstuck

When you're truly stuck, try these approaches:

- Start fresh. Sometimes it's faster to rebuild than to fix. Take what you learned and create a new version.
- Describe the problem to ChatGPT or Claude. Explain what you're trying to do, what's happening instead, and ask for suggestions.
- Search online. Someone has probably had a similar problem. Search error messages or describe the issue.
- Take a break. Seriously. Walk away for an hour or a day. Fresh eyes often see solutions immediately.
- Ask for help. Post in community forums for your tools. People are generally helpful.

Bonus: Prompt Library

Ready-to-Use Prompts

Here are prompts you can copy, customize, and use for common projects. Replace the bracketed sections with your details.

Personal Portfolio Website

Portfolio Prompt

Create a portfolio website for [YOUR NAME], a [YOUR PROFESSION]. Include: an About section with my bio, a Portfolio/Work section with [NUMBER] project cards showing title, description, and image, a Skills section listing my capabilities, and a Contact section with email and social links. Use [COLOR SCHEME] colors and a [modern/minimal/creative/professional] design. Must work well on phones.

Event Signup System

Event Registration Prompt

Build an event registration system for [ORGANIZATION NAME]. Admins can create events with name, date, time, location, description, and capacity limit. Users can browse upcoming events, register (collecting name, email, phone), and receive confirmation emails. Show a waitlist when events are full. Include a dashboard showing registration counts and attendee lists. Send reminder emails 24 hours before events.

Appointment Scheduler

Appointment Prompt

Create an appointment booking system for [BUSINESS TYPE]. I offer [SERVICES] lasting [DURATION]. Show my available slots for the next [TIMEFRAME]. Customers book by selecting a time, entering their name, email, phone, and any notes. Send confirmation and reminder emails. I need a dashboard to see my schedule, block off times, and manage bookings. Use

[AESTHETIC] design.

Simple CRM

CRM Prompt

Build a simple customer relationship manager for my
[BUSINESS TYPE]. Track contacts with name, email, phone,
company, and notes. Log interactions (calls, emails, meetings)
with dates and summaries. Add tags to categorize contacts.
Search and filter the contact list. Show a dashboard with recent
activity. Export contacts to CSV.

Habit Tracker

Habit Tracker Prompt

Create a daily habit tracking app. Track these habits: [LIST
YOUR HABITS]. Each day, tap to mark habits complete. Show
streaks for consecutive days. Display a weekly grid view. Send
customizable reminder notifications. Include a monthly
summary with statistics. Use [calm/energetic/minimal] design.

Inventory Tracker

Inventory Prompt

Build an inventory tracking system for [BUSINESS TYPE]. Add
items with name, SKU, category, quantity, minimum stock
level, cost, and photo. Update quantities when items are
received or sold. Alert when items fall below minimum levels.
Generate reports showing inventory value and low-stock items.
Search and filter by category.

Bonus: Frequently Asked Questions

Getting Started

Q: Do I really need zero coding experience?

A: Yes, really. The tools we use translate plain English into code. If you can describe what you want, you can build it. Some background helps (just like any skill), but it's not required.

Q: Which tool should I start with?

A: Lovable for most people. It has the gentlest learning curve and produces the most polished results. If you specifically want mobile apps, start with CreateAnything instead.

Q: How much will this cost me?

A: You can start completely free. All the tools have free tiers. Paid plans (typically $15-25/month) become worthwhile once you're building seriously or need more features. Budget $20-50/month once you're committed.

Q: How long until I can build real things?

A: You can build your first website in under an hour following this book. Simple apps in an afternoon. More complex projects in a few days. The learning curve is weeks, not months or years.

Technical Questions

Q: Where does my app actually live? How does it work?

A: Your app runs on servers managed by the platform (Lovable, Replit, etc.). They handle all the infrastructure. You get a URL that works anywhere. It's like how your email lives on Google's servers—you use it without managing the machines.

Q: What if the platform shuts down?

A: Most platforms let you export your code. If something happens, you can take your code and host it elsewhere. It's not ideal, but you're not locked in forever.

Q: Can I use my own domain name?

A: Yes! Most platforms support custom domains. You buy a domain separately (around $10-15/year from services like Namecheap or Google Domains) and connect it to your app.

Q: How do I handle sensitive data like passwords?

A: The platforms handle this for you. When you ask for 'user accounts,' the AI sets up secure authentication following best practices. For extra-sensitive applications (healthcare, finance), consult with professionals.

Building Questions

Q: What if the AI keeps getting it wrong?

A: Be more specific. If 'make a contact form' doesn't work well, try 'make a contact form with fields for name (required), email (required, validated), phone (optional), and message (required, at least 20 characters).' Specificity is your friend.

Q: How do I know if my prompt is good enough?

A: Ask yourself: Could someone else read this prompt and build exactly what I'm imagining? If there's room for interpretation, add more details. The five elements (what, who, why, features, aesthetic) help ensure completeness.

Q: Should I plan everything upfront or figure it out as I go?

A: A middle ground works best. Have a clear vision of the core functionality, but don't plan every detail. Build the basics, use them, then add features based on real experience.

Q: My app works but looks terrible. How do I fix the design?

A: Describe the aesthetic you want more specifically. Reference examples ('like Airbnb's clean style'). Ask for specific changes ('more whitespace,' 'softer colors,' 'larger text'). Sometimes starting a fresh design iteration is faster than fixing piecemeal.

Business Questions

Q: Can I really charge money for something I vibe-coded?

A: Absolutely. The value is in what your product does, not how it was built. Customers don't care whether code was written by hand or by AI—they care whether it solves their problem. Many successful SaaS products are built with no-code tools.

Q: What about support? What if customers have problems?

A: You provide support just like any business. Most issues will be user questions you can answer. For technical bugs, you debug through iteration—describe the problem to the AI and fix it. Complex issues might require help from the platform's support or community.

Q: Will people take my product seriously if they know it's vibe-coded?

A: They don't need to know, and most won't care. Results matter. But if asked, there's no shame—many professional developers use AI assistance now. Focus on the value you provide, not the implementation details.

Long-term Questions

Q: What happens when AI gets even better?

A: Your skills become more powerful, not obsolete. Better AI means you can build more complex things with the same effort. The core skills—clear communication, user understanding, iteration—will remain valuable regardless of tool improvements.

Q: Should I eventually learn 'real' coding?

A: Only if you want to. Many people build successful careers and businesses without ever writing traditional code. If you're curious, learning fundamentals can help—but it's not required. Choose based on your interests and goals, not obligation.

Q: What's the biggest mistake beginners make?

A: Starting too big. People imagine their dream app with 50 features and try to build it all at once. Start with the smallest useful version. Add features based on real use. Complexity is the enemy of completion.

> The best question to ask yourself isn't 'Can I build this?' It's 'What's the smallest version that would be useful?' Build that first.

One Last Thing

Thank you for reading this book. Seriously. In a world full of distractions, you chose to spend time learning something new. That matters.

The ability to build software is one of the most powerful skills in the modern world. Ideas that used to require teams and budgets can now be built by individuals with vision and persistence. You now have that power.

I'd love to see what you build. Share your creations on social media and tag me. Send me an email about your projects. Nothing makes me happier than seeing readers turn their ideas into reality.

Now close this book and go build something. Start today. Start small. Start now.

You've got this.

— Rebecca

Resources & Next Steps

Recommended Tools (Complete List)

Here's every tool mentioned in this book, organized by category:

AI Assistants (For Planning & Problem-Solving)

- ChatGPT (chat.openai.com) — General AI assistant, good for brainstorming
- Claude (claude.ai) — Deep reasoning, excellent for complex problems
- Claude Code (claude.ai) — Build complete projects with AI
- Perplexity (perplexity.ai) — AI-powered search and research

App Builders (No-Code)

- Lovable (lovable.dev) — Best for beginners, beautiful results
- Replit (replit.com) — Learning-focused, works on any device
- Bolt.new (bolt.new) — Fast prototyping
- v0 (v0.dev) — UI generation by Vercel

Mobile App Builders

- CreateAnything (createanything.com) — Native iOS/Android apps
- Draftbit (draftbit.com) — Mobile app builder
- Adalo (adalo.com) — No-code mobile apps

Advanced Tools

- Cursor (cursor.com) — AI-powered code editor
- VS Code (code.visualstudio.com) — Free code editor
- GitHub (github.com) — Code storage and collaboration

Common Integrations

- Stripe (stripe.com) — Payments
- SendGrid (sendgrid.com) — Email sending
- Twilio (twilio.com) — SMS messages
- Supabase (supabase.com) — Database + auth
- Cloudinary (cloudinary.com) — Image hosting
- PostHog (posthog.com) — Analytics

YouTube Channels to Follow

These creators share valuable content about vibe coding, no-code development, and building products:

- Starter Story — Interviews with founders and how they built their businesses, great for inspiration and practical insights on building products
- Mikey No Code — Focused on no-code and low-code development, shows you how to build real projects without traditional coding
- Edmund Yong — Covers AI tools, automation, and building with new technology, practical tutorials you can follow along with
- Chris Koerner — Explores AI tools and how to use them effectively for building and business, stays on top of the latest developments

Subscribe to these channels and check in regularly. The vibe coding landscape changes fast, and these creators do a great job staying current.

Communities to Join

Connect with other builders:

- Reddit: r/nocode, r/SideProject, r/Entrepreneur
- Twitter/X: Follow #buildinpublic and #nocode hashtags
- Discord: Most tools have official Discord servers
- Indie Hackers (indiehackers.com) — Community of solo founders

• Product Hunt (producthunt.com) — Discover and launch products

Books for Further Learning

If you want to go deeper:

• 'The Mom Test' by Rob Fitzpatrick — How to talk to customers
• 'Don't Make Me Think' by Steve Krug — User experience basics
• 'The Lean Startup' by Eric Ries — Building products iteratively
• 'Make' by Pieter Levels — Bootstrapping indie products

Stay Updated

The vibe coding landscape changes rapidly. Stay current:

• Follow tool announcements (new features launch constantly)
• Subscribe to newsletters like 'No-Code Exits' and 'Indie Hackers'
• Watch YouTube for tutorials on new tools and techniques
• Experiment regularly—try new tools as they emerge

Your 30-Day Challenge

Here's a challenge to cement your skills:

Week 1: Build something for yourself that you'll use daily

Week 2: Build something for a family member or friend

Week 3: Build something for your work or community

Week 4: Build something that could potentially make money

By the end of 30 days, you'll have four projects and a clear sense of what you enjoy building most.

The only way to get better at building is to build. Start today. Start small. Start now.

Quick Reference Guide

The Five Elements of a Great Prompt

1. **Context** — What type of project is this?

2. **Audience** — Who will use it?

3. **Purpose** — What problem does it solve?

4. **Features** — What should it do?

5. **Aesthetic** — How should it look and feel?

Iteration Phrases That Work

- Make it more modern / minimal / playful / professional

  - Add a feature that lets users...

  - The [specific thing] isn't working, can you fix it?

  - Can you make this mobile-friendly?

  - Simplify the navigation

  - Add more white space

  - Make the buttons more prominent

When Things Go Wrong

If it won't load: Ask the AI to check for syntax errors

If it looks broken: Ask to fix the CSS styling

If a feature doesn't work: Describe exactly what should happen vs. what is happening

If you're stuck: Start a new conversation with a clearer prompt

About the Author

Rebecca M. Stallworth is an art teacher by day and a collegiate history instructor by night. But her real passion is building—businesses, systems, and tools that create freedom.

A serial entrepreneur, Rebecca runs multiple income streams including an Etsy shop, Airbnb hosting, and now software products built through vibe coding. She homeschooled her son Joshua for nine years, during which she tagged along to his Apple camps and discovered her love for technology and building things online.

Rebecca serves as Deputy Commander for Civil Air Patrol's Andrews Composite Squadron, where she helps develop the next generation of leaders. She holds a Master's in History from Jackson State University and is currently pursuing a Master of Public Health.

Born in Jackson, Mississippi, Rebecca now lives in Prince George's County, Maryland with her two huskies, Macy and Lucy. Her son Joshua is a business major and founder of Gosh Josh Cookies.

Rebecca writes about building multiple income streams, entrepreneurship, and designing a life of freedom.

Connect with Rebecca:

Website: **secondchaptermoney.com**

Etsy: **passiveprofitsstudio.etsy.com**

Pinterest: **pinterest.com/secondchaptermoney**

Medium: **medium.com/@rmstallworth**

TikTok: **@rebeccamstallworth**